Kids' Book of Clouds & Sky

Written and Photographed
by
Frank Staub

Sterling Publishing Co., Inc.
New York

For Marsha,
who keeps her head above the clouds

"Under a cumulonimbus cloud, Tucson, AZ"

NOAA: photograph courtesy of the National Oceanic
and Atmospheric Administration

Library of Congress Cataloging-in-Publishing Data Available

10 9 8 7 6 5 4 3 2 1

Published in paperback in 2005 by Sterling Publishing Co., Inc.
387 Park Avenue South, New York, N.Y. 10016
© 2003 by Frank Staub
Distributed in Canada by Sterling Publishing
% Canadian Manda Group, 165 Dufferin Street,
Toronto, Ontario, Canada M6K 3H6
Distributed in Great Britain and Europe by Chris Lloyd at Orca Book Services,
Stanley House, Fleets Lane, Poole BH15 3AJ, England
Distributed in Australia by Capricorn Link (Australia) Pty. Ltd.
P.O. Box 704, Windsor, NSW 2756, Australia

Printed in China
All rights reserved

Sterling ISBN 0-8069-7879-1 Hardcover
        ISBN 1-4027-2806-9 Paperback

For information about custom editions, special sales, premium and
corporate purchases, please contact Sterling Special Sales
Department at 800-805-5489 or specialsales@sterlingpub.com.

Contents

What Can I Tell from the Sky?

When you understand the things you see in the sky, you'll notice them more often, and enjoy them more, too.

Mountain climbers and boaters need to know what the sky can tell them, because mountaintops and the open sea are dangerous places to be during storms.

Since the beginning of time, people have looked to the sky with wonder and respect. Our ancient ancestors thought rainbows, lightning, comets, and other sky signs were the work of gods and spirits. Today, people often "read the sky" to forecast the weather. You may learn a storm is coming because of certain kinds of clouds, the color of the evening, or how clear the air is. But pleasure may be the best reason to learn what the sky has to say. Knowing what fog is, or what causes sunbeams, or how to tell the difference between stars and planets can be fun.

The atmosphere coats the earth like a clear skin about 80 miles (128km) thick, although a small number of air molecules occur hundreds of miles up.

Some of the most abundant large particles in the atmosphere, sea salt, get tossed into the air when ocean waves break.

We see only a small part of the atmosphere curving above us, and call it the sky.

What Is the Sky Made of?

When we look at the daytime sky we see the earth's atmosphere. Just as the ocean is full of water, the atmosphere is full of **air**. Air is a mixture of gas molecules. A molecule is the smallest part of something that still has the characteristics of that thing. A gas is a substance that expands in all directions, unlike a solid that has a definite shape, or a liquid that flows on a surface. Air is made up of many different kinds of gases—such as nitrogen, oxygen, carbon dioxide, and **water vapor**, the gas form of water. Other larger particles are mixed in, too—dust, soot from fires, pollen from plants, ash shot from volcanoes, salt from the sea, and tiny drops of water.

Why Is the Sky Blue?

The first thing most people wonder about the sky is why it is blue. Why does it have any color at all? After all, the gases in the atmosphere are usually invisible. To start with, sunlight is actually made up of different colors. Did you ever see the way a prism bends and separates sunlight into colors? Air does something like that. The blue part of the light strikes gas molecules in the air. This bends the blue and scatters it, flooding the sky with blue.

The daytime sky is like a big blue curtain hiding the stars. But the moon is often bright enough to shine through.

If the air didn't scatter sunlight, the daytime sky would appear black, just like at night.

EXPERIMENT

Separating the Colors of Sunlight

Place a jar of water beside a window so that the sun shines directly through the water onto a white paper. Watch the colors appear. You can do the same thing in a dark room, by shining a flashlight through the water.

Light coming through a jar of water breaks into the colors red, orange, yellow, green, blue, indigo, and violet. All of them together make the sunlight look white.

The higher you look in the sky, the darker it is, because there are fewer particles up high to scatter the light.

Where the land is low, you can see how pale the lower sky is, because most of the large particles in the air are close to the earth.

Why Is the Sky Light Blue Down Low and Dark Blue Up High?

The sky is darker blue after a storm, because rain washes dust from the air.

Water drops, dust, and other large particles in the atmosphere bend and scatter all the colors in sunlight. The scattered light is white, and it combines with the blue light scattered by the gas molecules. The white-blue combination creates a paler shade of blue. Gravity holds most of these gas molecules and larger particles close to the earth. If you took off in a spaceship, there would be less air as you went higher up. The sky would become darker. A few hundred miles above the earth, there would be no air at all to scatter the sunlight, and the sky would be black.

The more large particles there are in the sky, the lighter the shade of blue.

If there are high clouds above a clear sky on the western horizon, get ready for a pretty sky after the sun sets.

As the day begins, the color just above the horizon changes from red to orange to yellow to blue. As the day ends, the color change is reversed.

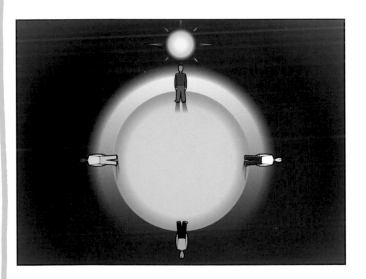

If dense clouds block the sun, all the colors, including the red, scatter, and the sky looks gray.

When you see red in the sky at day's end, people farther west still see the sky as blue. For them, the sun is still high in the sky. What you see as a setting sun is sunrise for people even farther west. The sun hasn't reached people on the other side of the world at all. For them, it's night.

Why Does the Sky's Color Change at the Beginning and End of the Day?

When the sun is near the horizon—the boundary between earth and sky— its light travels through more atmosphere to reach us than when it is high in the sky. This longer path causes sunlight to hit more molecules and other particles. Most of the colors bend and scatter so much that we can't see them. Often, however, the warm colors, such as red, yellow, and orange, scatter very little. They shine through onto the clouds and sky.

Why Does the Sun Seem to Change Shape as It Rises and Sets?

To see the sun change shape as it rises or sets, the horizon must be low and flat, like on the prairie or the ocean.

Sunrise is that instant when the sun's upper edge touches the horizon. Sunset is that instant when the sun's upper edge drops below the horizon. The thicker atmosphere that the sunlight passes through just after sunrise and just before sunset makes the sun look bigger. Plus, light from the bottom of the sun's disk travels through just a little more atmosphere than light from the top. As a result, the atmosphere bends light from the bottom of the disk slightly more than it bends light from the top. This slight difference makes the sun appear less round as it crosses the horizon.

Amazingly, the sun is below the horizon when you see a sunrise or sunset. At these times, the atmosphere between you and the sun is so thick that it actually bends the sun's image around the curve of the earth and into your view. This makes the sun appear to rise two minutes earlier than the true time when it crosses the horizon, and set two minutes later.

When you first notice the morning sun, the actual sunrise may have already taken place. Hills, mountains, trees, or buildings may have blocked it.

It takes several minutes for the sun's disk to completely appear after sunrise, and several minutes to disappear before sunset.

11

What Time Is Twilight?

When the sun is just below the horizon, dust and other particles in the atmosphere catch its light and bounce it up into the part of the sky we can see. The result is **twilight**—that time when the sun isn't in the sky but there is still light. Twilight is shortest at the equator, an imaginary line around the earth's middle, because sunlight passes through less light-scattering air to reach the earth's surface. The light between sunset and full night is called **afterglow**. Light in the sky between full night and sunrise is called **morning glow**.

Without particles in the air to bounce light above the horizon, the sky would be black from sunset to sunrise.

Twilight lasts from about 25 to 40 minutes in most parts of the world.

The length of twilight increases as you move away from the equator, because more sunlight scatters on its longer path through the atmosphere.

Is It True that You Can Tell Direction from the Sun?

The sun always rises somewhere in the east. It always sets somewhere in the west. At midday, the sun is roughly halfway through its journey across the sky. Before noon, the sun is in the eastern side of the sky, and after that it's in the west.

The exact path the sun takes from east to west depends on two things: The time of year, and where you live in relation to the equator. The equator divides the earth into two halves, or **hemispheres**. One half is called the Northern Hemisphere, and the other is called the Southern Hemisphere.

During summer in the Northern Hemisphere, the sun rises in the northeast and sets in the northwestern part of the sky.

During a Northern Hemisphere winter, the sun's path is in the southern half of the sky. It rises in the southeast and sets in the southwest.

Just the opposite happens in the Southern Hemisphere.

Danger! You could damage your eyes when you look at the sun if it's more than a short distance above the horizon.

On a winter morning in the Northern Hemisphere, the sun is in the southeastern sky. It sets in the southwest.

On a summer afternoon in the Northern Hemisphere, the sun is in the northwestern sky. It rises in the northeast.

In places that lie on the equator, such as the island of Borneo, the sun rises closer to due east or directly east, and sets closer to due west than anywhere else.

What Makes Air Humid?

Of all the gases in the atmosphere, water vapor has the biggest effect on what we see in the sky. Liquid water changes into the gas water vapor when it evaporates. Water vapor is what makes the air humid or moist. The amount of water vapor in the air is the **humidity**. When the humidity is so high that the air can't hold any more water vapor, we say the air is "saturated."

Heat causes evaporation to go faster. Also, warm air holds more water vapor than cold air. That's partly why the atmosphere near the equator contains so much water vapor.

Water vapor changes back into liquid water when it condenses, which it does only if it has a surface to condense onto. That's why water forms on the outside of a glass of cold juice on a hot day. The glass is the surface for condensation.

EXPERIMENT

Saturation

Put a few drops of water in a clear plastic jar and close the jar tightly. If you can still see water drops in the jar after about an hour, the air is saturated. If the water drops are gone, they have evaporated and the air in the jar may not be saturated: it can probably hold more water vapor. Now put the jar in the refrigerator for about ten minutes. As the air cools, it can't hold as much water. Water drops will appear on the sides of the jar as the water vapor condenses back into liquid water. Now put the jar in the sun. As the air in the jar gets warmer, the water drops will evaporate and disappear, because warm air holds more water vapor than cold air.

Whether the air in the jar is hot or cold, if you can see water drops in it, the air is saturated.

Although most water vapor evaporates from the oceans, some also comes from ponds, lakes, rivers, streams, puddles, plants, animals, and other sources of liquid.

EXPERIMENT

Evaporation and Heat

Dissolve some salt in water. Then pour the water into two plates. Place one plate in the sun and one in the shade. Check the plates every few hours. As time passes, the water evaporates, but the salt stays behind. You'll see the salt appear sooner in the plate in the sun than in the plate in the shade, because heat speeds up the evaporation.

The sun's warmth increases the rate of evaporation.

Humid air over the ocean near the equator might be 4% water vapor (left). But dry air over a desert might be only 1% water vapor (right).

The water droplets in a cloud condense around particles such as specks of dust, soot, sea salt, or plant pollen.

Air becomes saturated and clouds form when enough water evaporates into water vapor, or when the temperature of the air drops.

The point above the earth where rising air cools to the dew point and clouds form is sometimes called the "condensation level."

What Are Clouds?

As saturated air cools, some of its water vapor condenses into tiny water droplets. When you see your breath on a cold day, it's because water vapor has condensed onto large particles in the air and become water droplets. If the air is very cold, ice crystals form instead of water droplets. A cloud is a collection of billions of water droplets, ice crystals, or both.

The temperature at which water vapor starts to condense into water droplets is called the **dew point**. When its temperature drops below its dew point, the air has become saturated and too cool to hold all of its water vapor. That extra water vapor condenses onto particles in the air and turns into water droplets or ice crystals to form clouds. The more water vapor in the air, the higher the dew point, and the more likely it is that we will have clouds.

The water droplets and ice crystals in clouds don't fall because upward moving air currents hold them up.

Air may cool down enough to form clouds if it rises higher into the sky.

Most clouds are white, because water droplets and ice crystals usually reflect all the colors in sunlight equally.

Humid air, which contains lots of water vapor, has a higher dew point and will produce more clouds than dry air, which contains little water vapor.

EXPERIMENT

Measuring the Dew Point

Cover the bottom of a jar with ice cubes. Hold a thermometer just inside the mouth of the jar. Don't let the thermometer touch the ice. When water drops condense on the jar, note the temperature. This is the dew point. If all the air in the room were to suddenly cool down to that temperature, a cloud might form.

Making a Cloud

Making a Cloud with Powder

Put an inch (2.5cm) of water in a big jar. Cover the jar mouth with a piece of balloon that has burst. Place a book on the balloon to hold it in place. Wait 15 minutes to allow some of the water to evaporate into water vapor. Remove the book and balloon, drop in a little talcum powder, and quickly replace the balloon over the jar. Wrap a rubber band around the rim to hold the balloon in place. Now press down on the balloon with your fist so that it sags a little into the jar. This compresses the air and moves the molecules closer together. When air is compressed, it gets warmer. The warmer air can hold more water vapor. After about 20 seconds, quickly remove your fist. Now the air is no longer compressed. It cools and can't hold as much water vapor. The particles of powder provide surfaces for the extra water vapor to condense onto and form water droplets. You have made a cloud.

Making a Cloud with Hot Water and Ice

Pour an inch (2.5cm) of hot water into a jar and put the lid on. The air in the jar will soon contain lots of water vapor, because the hot water will evaporate. Remove the lid and put a strainer over the mouth of the jar. Fill the strainer with ice cubes. The ice cubes will cause the temperature in the jar to go down. As the air in the jar gets cooler, it will become saturated. Then the water vapor will condense into water droplets. Once again you have made a cloud.

Temperatures don't usually drop much when clouds stick around after sunset and through the night.

Daytime temperatures rise faster when there are few clouds to block the sun's warmth.

The saying "Clear moon, frost soon" means the moon isn't blocked by clouds that would hold down the day's heat and keep frost from forming.

Overcast days during the winter are often very cold.

Do Clouds Affect Temperature?

You know that when the sun shines, the air usually gets warmer. You also know that a heavy, daytime cloud cover blocks sunlight and keeps temperatures down. But you may not know that just the opposite happens at night. Clouds covering the nighttime sky act like a blanket. They hold down the heat that the earth absorbed during the day, and keep it from escaping into space. However, on clear or mostly clear nights you can expect cooler temperatures because there are fewer clouds to block heat from drifting back into the sky. That's why clear nights are usually cooler than cloudy nights.

Clouds that form in hot air may produce more rain than clouds in cold air, because hot, saturated air contains more water vapor.

Raindrops are so big and heavy that the little air currents in a cloud can't hold them up. So they fall to earth.

Rain clouds are dark because, unlike water droplets that reflect white light, raindrops absorb sunlight.

What Causes Rain and Snow?

Rain, snow, and other forms of water that fall from the sky are called **precipitation**. When water droplets moving about in a cloud bump into each other, they combine to form bigger droplets. After about a million droplets combine, a raindrop forms.

When parts of a rain cloud are cold enough, some of the droplets turn into tiny ice crystals. Water droplets bump into the ice crystals and freeze onto them, making the crystals bigger. When an ice crystal grows close to the size of the period at the end of this sentence, it starts to fall as a snowflake. Snowflakes grow larger as they fall and crash into other snowflakes and more water droplets. If the temperature of the air near the ground is cold, we have

Dark clouds that bring rain and snow often have the word "nimbus" or "nimbo" added to their names. "Nimbus" is the Latin word for "rain-bearing" or "snow-bearing."

snow. But if the snowflakes fall through warmer air, they may melt into rain.

Sometimes the air at ground level is below freezing while the air higher up is not. Raindrops then freeze as they touch the cold earth. A storm that produces this freezing rain is called an ice storm. If the low layer of cold air is thick enough, the raindrops freeze into pellets of ice before reaching the ground. The ice pellets are called sleet.

Rain or snow falling from a cloud may evaporate before reaching the earth. The precipitation then hangs from the cloud in streaks called **virga**.

Virga are common in deserts where precipitation evaporates quickly in the dry air before reaching the ground.

How High Are the Clouds?

The distance from the earth to the bottom of a cloud is called its altitude. It can be hard to figure out. But recognizing the kind of cloud you're looking at is easier. Scientists have names for about 100 different cloud types. Some are high and some are low. The two most common low altitude clouds are **stratus clouds** and **cumulus clouds**. Stratus clouds are flat. The base of a stratus cloud may be from ground level up to about one-half mile (0.8km). Cumulus clouds are puffy. If the humidity is high, a cumulus cloud's low point may be about 3,000 feet (900m). However, cumulus clouds in dry regions such as deserts sometimes have bases as high as 10,000 feet (3,000m). This is still low compared to some clouds.

This mountain towers 3,000 feet (900m) above the valley floor, so the cloud's altitude must be about 1,500 feet (450m).

Cumulus clouds look like puffy heaps or piles of cotton. "Cumulus" is the Latin word for "heap."

Stratus clouds are spread flat in layers. "Stratus" means "layered" in Latin.

Both stratus clouds (right) and cumulus clouds (bottom) are closest to the ground in the morning and rise as the air warms up later in the day.

23

Stratus clouds form what many people call "leaden skies," because they often make the sky gray, the color of lead.

What Makes the Sky Overcast?

When the sky is overcast, it's usually covered with dull, gray, stratus clouds. Stratus develop when a layer of air cools to its dew point. The air layer is stable. That means it isn't churned up by lots of air currents. A stratus cloud may be small and cover only part of the sky—or it may extend 100 miles (160km). Sometimes you can see the sun or moon through a stratus cloud, and sometimes you can't.

A stratus cloud may bring some drizzle but not rain. For that you need a **nimbostratus** cloud, which is darker, and its bottom isn't usually as smooth. Stratus clouds often turn into nimbostratus.

Sometimes raindrops evaporate as they fall, and saturate the air below a nimbostratus or other rain cloud with water vapor. Then the water vapor condenses into little cloud pieces called **scuds**.

The bottom of a stratus cloud may cover the tops of tall trees or buildings. Or it may be even lower.

Scud clouds below nimbostratus and other rain clouds look like cloud scraps.

If the air containing a stratus cloud becomes less stable, rising air currents may break up the stratus layer into smaller stratus cloud patches.

Precipitation makes the bottom of a nimbostratus cloud look blurry.

The bottom of a cumulus cloud is usually dark because the cloud is too thick for much sunlight to pass through.

When air sinks and warms up, the water droplets it contains may evaporate. The spaces between clouds are where air sinks and droplets evaporate.

Dry air around a cumulus cloud causes parts of the cloud to evaporate.

Updrafts pushing on the sides and top of a cumulus cloud cause the cloud's shape to change constantly.

When air warms up and rises, it can make faraway objects look like they're shimmering.

At day's end or during the night as the earth cools off, thermals weaken and cumulus clouds shrink and disappear.

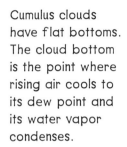

Cumulus clouds have flat bottoms. The cloud bottom is the point where rising air cools to its dew point and its water vapor condenses.

How Do Cumulus Clouds Form on Sunny Days?

You often see puffy, flat-bottomed, cumulus clouds on warm, sunny afternoons. A "fair weather cumulus" starts to form when the sun heats the earth and the earth heats the air above it. As the air gets warmer, the air molecules move farther apart. With more space between the molecules, the air becomes lighter and rises into the sky. A rising ball of warm air is called a **thermal**. Thermals may be as small as 65 feet (20m) wide or as big as hundreds of feet across. Hang gliders and soaring birds, such as hawks, eagles, and vultures, ride thermals high into the sky. Thermals can cause airplane passengers to have bumpy rides. When there are lots of thermals and rising air currents, the air is unstable.

As a thermal rises, it cools. When the air in a thermal cools off enough to reach the dew point, its water vapor condenses into water droplets to form a cloud. Inside the cloud, air keeps rising as updrafts. Updrafts push out the cloud's top and sides to give a cumulus cloud its puffy shape.

Two or more cumulonimbus clouds may combine to produce a very violent storm.

The top of a cumulonimbus cloud may tower up to eleven miles (18km) above the earth.

Updrafts puff out the top of a growing cumulonimbus cloud like a giant piece of popcorn that keeps on popping.

What Kind of Cloud Brings Sudden, Hard Rain Showers?

If cumulus clouds produce rain or snow, they go by a new name: **cumulonimbus**. Cumulonimbus clouds grow tall on hot, humid days as large thermals with lots of moisture rise into the sky, or when large areas of cold air wedge beneath large areas of warm air. As raindrops fall through a tall cumulonimbus cloud, they create downward moving air currents called downdrafts. Updrafts push the raindrops back up. The raindrops travel up and down inside the cloud, pushed by updrafts and downdrafts. With each round trip, they collide, combine, and get bigger. In the cold, upper part of the cloud they may freeze into little ice balls called **hailstones**. Hailstones grow larger as more drops freeze onto them. When a raindrop or hailstone gets so heavy that the updrafts can't push it up any longer, it falls to earth.

Some storms from cumulonimbus clouds are less than a mile (1.6km) across and move through quickly.

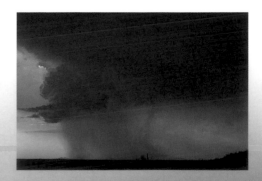

This cumulonimbus is too far away to see its base. But you do see its anvil because the cloud is so high.

A blacksmith's anvil is a big, steel block that is very wide at the top, like the top of this cumulonimbus.

Mammatus are usually smooth and rounded.

Eventually, downdrafts cut off the updrafts and a cumulonimbus disappears, leaving only the wispy, anvil top.

Why Are Cumulonimbus Clouds Often Swollen at the Top and Bulging at the Bottom?

The air temperature is below freezing at the top of a tall cumulonimbus, so the cloud top is made of ice crystals instead of water droplets. The strong winds at these high altitudes may cause the icy cloud top of a cumulonimbus to spread out into a fanlike structure called an **anvil**. The name comes from the anvil that blacksmiths pound metal on. Strong downdrafts within a big cumulonimbus may push the cloud base down into baglike bulges called **mammatus**.

What Causes Lightning and Thunder?

A sky crowded with rapidly growing cumulus clouds could produce lightning later in the day as the clouds turn into cumulonimbus.

Updrafts from the 2002 Hayman forest fire in Colorado produced big cumulonimbus clouds and lightning.

The top of a cumulonimbus cloud has a positive electrical charge. The cloud bottom has a negative charge. Positive and negative charges attract each other. As the charges become stronger, the attraction between the positive at the top and the negative at the bottom grows and grows. Something has to give, and it does when a giant spark we call lightning jumps the space separating the charges. If the earth's surface is positively charged, lightning may also jump from the negative cloud bottom to the earth.

How hot is lightning? Air temperatures along a lightning bolt's path shoot up instantly to about 18,000 degrees Fahrenheit (10,000 degrees Celsius). That's hotter than

Lightning strikes about 10,000 people each year. Most survive. Many don't.

There's five times more lightning within clouds and between clouds than between the clouds and the ground.

the sun! The tremendous heat causes the air to explode. We hear the explosion as thunder. Rainstorms from cumulonimbus clouds are often called thunderstorms, and thunder-producing cumulonimbus clouds are sometimes called **thunderheads**.

You always see lightning before you hear thunder because light travels a hundred thousand times faster than sound. It takes the sound of the thunder five seconds to travel just one mile. Use this fact to tell how far away the storm is. The instant you see lightning, start reciting "One thunder, two thunder, three thunder, four thunder . . ." , until you hear thunder. Each count is about one second. Divide the number you stop at by five to get the distance in miles (divide by three for kilometers). Then use the 30-30 rule: If you count 30 seconds or less, the lightning is no more than six miles away. So get inside fast and stay there until 30 minutes after the last clap of thunder. People have been struck by lightning from clouds over ten miles away.

Lightning may strike the same place again and again—especially a high place.

The quiet glow people call "heat lightning" is caused by lightning that is too far away to see the actual bolt or hear the thunder.

A big bolt of lightning may look like it's many feet thick. But it's actually only about one inch (2.54cm) wide.

Jim Peaco, Yellowstone National Park

31

What Are the Most Dangerous Storms?

Sometimes the updrafts in a big cumulonimbus cloud turn in a rotating pattern. When this happens, the cloud produces especially big, powerful, and long-lasting thunderstorms called **supercells**. Some supercells, and clusters of cumulonimbus clouds, give rise to the most violent storms on earth—**tornadoes**. The water droplets in these funnel-shaped, killer clouds are pushed around and around by rapidly twisting winds that spin out from the cloud bottom. Sometimes a funnel cloud reaches the earth's surface where it can uproot trees, rip buildings to pieces, and lift trains off their tracks. A funnel cloud that reaches down to an ocean or lake is called a **waterspout**.

The rotating winds in a tornado are the fastest on the earth's surface—up to 300 miles (480km) per hour. Fortunately, tornadoes don't cover a large area and they don't last long.

Most of the world's tornadoes occur on the plains of central North America during spring and summer. This is a time when warm, moist air from the southeast, cold air from the north, and dry air from the southwest all come together. The combination is ideal for tornadoes. It's why the region is nicknamed "Tornado Alley."

NOAA

The point where a funnel cloud touches the ground may be narrower than a city block or wider than a sports stadium.

NOAA

Like any cloud, a waterspout is mostly water droplets. Spray stirred up from the surface appears at the spout's base.

Mammatus such as these may appear before a funnel cloud forms.

Steady winds shape some stratocumulus clouds into long rows.

Compared to the relatively smooth bottoms of stratus clouds, the bottoms of stratocumulus clouds are bumpy.

Stratocumulus clouds are thin, just as stratus clouds are.

Like stratus clouds, stratocumulus spread out as layers.

What Clouds Look Like Stratus and Cumulus Combined?

These lumpy, wavy, or slightly puffy cloud layers are part stratus and part cumulus. And their name says so—**stratocumulus**. Like both stratus clouds and cumulus clouds, stratocumulus are low, water droplet clouds occurring from 500 feet (150m) up to 5,000 feet (1,500m) above the ground. They may form when air currents break up stratus clouds, or when cumulus clouds spread out flat. If rain or snow falls from a stratocumulus cloud, the cloud becomes a nimbostratus.

33

Cirrus clouds are well over three miles (4,827m) above the earth.

High altitude winds of 100 mph (160km/h) or more often twist cirrus cloud ice crystals into curling strands. "Cirrus" means "curl" in Latin.

What Are the High, Thin, Feathery Clouds?

Thin, wispy clouds that look like shredded feathers are **cirrus** clouds. These clouds are often called "mares' tails" because they look like the tails of horses. Unlike the low stratus, cumulus, and stratocumulus clouds, cirrus clouds are high—no less than 18,000 feet (5,500m) above the earth. Because the air at such altitudes is freezing cold, the water vapor that gives rise to cirrus clouds turns directly into ice crystals, not water droplets.

You may see cirrus clouds during long periods of mostly clear skies. But sometimes cirrus clouds are early warning signs that rain or snow is on the way.

Except around sunrise and sunset, cirrus clouds are white because their ice crystals reflect all the colors in sunlight equally.

Ice crystals falling from cirrus clouds often stream away at angles because they fall to levels where the winds are slower.

34

What Are the Long, White Clouds Behind Jet Airplanes?

Water vapor shoots out the back of a jet engine with the hot gases of the engine exhaust. Many jets fly higher than 30,000 feet (9,000m). When the jet exhaust strikes the cold, high-altitude air, its water vapor freezes into ice crystals. The ice crystals trail behind the zooming jet as a thin, white line called a **contrail**. The name is a combination of the words "condensation" and "trail." A contrail is like an artificial cirrus cloud—very high, all white, and made of ice crystals.

If contrails don't evaporate right away, they get thicker as the wind pushes and spreads out the ice crystals.

Many jets fly so high you can't see them. All you see are their contrails.

Contrails appear to be behind cumulus clouds, because jets fly higher than most cumulus clouds.

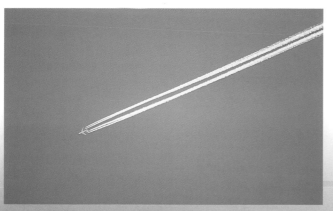

Contrails tend to be thicker and longer-lasting in humid air. In dry air, they are thin and evaporate quickly.

Are There Other High Clouds Made of Ice Crystals?

Cirrostratus clouds may form thin sheets across the sky.

There are other clouds made of ice crystals instead of water droplets. Some are thin, veil-like sheets or bands. They are called **cirrostratus** clouds. Others are puffy patches that look like flocks of tiny sheep. These are **cirrocumulus**. Any cloud with the word "cirro" in its name is a high cloud. Like cirrus clouds, cirrostratus and cirrocumulus both occur above 18,000 feet (5,500m).

As with any stratus-type or layered cloud, cirrostratus clouds form in stable air with few up and down currents. The calm layer of cirrostratus ice crystals may bend light to form a big ring or **halo** around the sun or moon. Sometimes bright spots called **sundogs** sit on opposite sides of the halo.

Cirrocumulus clouds form in less stable air with more up and down air movements. Water vapor in the rising air condenses into little cloud islands made of ice crystals. These clouds are said to create a "mackerel sky," because they look like the scales of a mackerel fish.

Like their cirrus cousins, both cirrostratus and cirrocumulus produce no precipitation. But also like cirrus clouds, they may sometimes be early warning signs of rain or snow.

A cirrostratus cloud may be so thin that a halo is the only way you know the cloud is there.

36

In the spaces between cirrocumulus cloud islands, the air sinks and the ice crystals turn back into water vapor.

Another name for sun dogs is "mock suns," because they look like extra suns. Sun dogs are often colorful.

Cirrostratus cloud bands that seem to shoot out from one spot are actually the same distance apart along their entire lengths.

Cirrocumulus patches or ripples don't usually cover the entire sky.

A smooth, dull, gray or blue-gray altostratus layer is thicker than a white cirrostratus.

Altostratus clouds may block the sun completely, or the sun may shine through as a bright, fuzzy ball called a "wet sun."

Are There In-Between Clouds—Neither High nor Low?

Cumulus, stratus, and stratocumulus are low clouds. Cirrus, cirrostratus, and cirrocumulus are high clouds. Clouds at middle levels are called **altostratus** and **altocumulus**. They occur between 6,500 feet and 16,500 feet (2,000m and 5,000m). The air at such altitudes is often below freezing. So these in-between clouds contain ice crystals as well as water droplets. Both altostratus and altocumulus may, at times, be early warnings that wet weather is on the way.

Like any stratus-type cloud, altostratus form when a stable air layer rises and cools to the dew point. Water vapor in the rising air then condenses to form a broad cloud layer.

Don't look directly at a corona (left) or iridescence (right). The sun could damage your eyes!

Altocumulus islands appear larger than cirrocumulus, because altocumulus are lower. Unlike cirrocumulus that are always white, altocumulus are always shaded with gray.

Like most cumulus-type clouds, altocumulus form in air made unstable by rising air currents. Water vapor in the rising air cools to the dew point to form cloud islands that take on a variety of shapes. As with cirrocumulus clouds, a sky full of altocumulus cloud islands is called a "mackerel sky."

When the water droplets in altocumulus and altostratus clouds are all about the same size, they may bend light to form a **corona**, a small, bright, and often colorful disk around the sun or moon. Or, the cloud's droplets may bend sunlight to form **iridescence**, a patch of color on the cloud's bottom.

Sometimes altostratus clouds stretch out into a layer of long rows or bands.

Wave clouds may form whenever air rises and falls in a wave pattern.

High winds flowing through layers of dry air and moist air piled on top of each other create stacks of wave clouds.

When wave clouds form to one side of a mountain, it is always the downwind side—not the side the wind is coming from.

What Clouds Look Like Flying Saucers?

A wave-type cloud that looks like a cap may form on a mountaintop when winds flow up one side and down the other.

Sometimes when saucer-shaped objects appear in the sky, people imagine that they're spaceships from other planets. Some of these "flying saucers" may actually be special kinds of altocumulus clouds called **wave clouds**. Like saucers, wave clouds have a smooth, streamlined shape. They form when winds between about 6,500 feet and 16,500 feet (2,000m and 5,000m) flow in up-and-down wave patterns, often over a mountain. The air rises up into a wave the same way a stream forms a wave when it flows over a rock. The high part of the wave is colder than the low part. So water vapor in the air flowing through the upper wave condenses into a cloud. As the air moves on to the lower and warmer part of the wave, the water droplets may evaporate if the air is warm enough. Then the cloud is limited to the upper part of the wave. The dew point in the lower part is too low for a cloud to form.

Strong winds form wave clouds, but the clouds move little or not at all.

Because of their rounded forms shaped by the wind, some wave clouds are called "lenticulars" meaning "lens-shaped."

What If I See More than One Kind of Cloud?

You'll often see more than one kind of cloud at different levels. You may also see one cloud type blending into another type at the same level. When such things happen, it's called a mixed sky. The best times for identifying the different cloud types in a mixed sky are early and late in the day, because the low sun makes the clouds stand out.

When the lower clouds are cumulus, look through the spaces between them at what's higher up. But if a stratus or nimbostratus is overhead, it will block your view of what's at the mid and upper levels. There may be a cumulonimbus up there. Then, driving rain and possibly thunder and lightning will let you know soon enough.

Cumulus and cirrus clouds often occur together during good weather. But sometimes a mixed sky means there's so much moisture in the air that rain or snow is possible. Clouds at different levels blowing in different directions are a good sign that a storm is on the way.

Can you identify the clouds in these pictures of mixed skies?
The answers are at the bottom of the pages.

2.

1.

1. Dawn with cirrostratus above stratocumulus. 2. Cirrocumulus above cumulus.

3.

4.

5.

6.

7.

8.

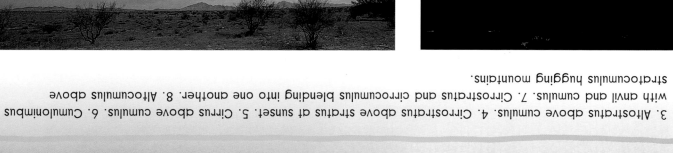

3. Altostratus above cumulus. 4. Cirrostratus above stratus at sunset. 5. Cirrus above cumulus. 6. Cumulonimbus with anvil and cumulus. 7. Cirrostratus and cirrocumulus blending into one another. 8. Altocumulus above stratocumulus hugging mountains.

43

From a distance, it's easy to see that this fog layer is really a stratus cloud on the ground.

Fog can make driving dangerous because it limits visibility.

A valley fog evaporates or "burns off" quickly as the sun comes out and warms the air.

What Are Fog and Haze?

Fog is a cloud on the ground. It forms the same way other clouds do. Air cools to its dew point and water vapor condenses into water droplets. But the air doesn't rise. Fog often forms when warm, moist air blows onto a cold land surface. The land cools the air to its dew point and fog forms.

Fog may also appear when air travels up the side of a mountain and cools to its dew point. Because the fog forms as the wind blows up the slope, this type of fog is called an "upslope" fog.

Cool air often tends to slide downhill into the valleys and other low-lying areas. If the air continues to cool to its dew point, valley fog develops.

44

Fog often forms over rivers and lakes and in humid valleys.

Winter fogs may form when warm, moist air blows to a place where the temperature is lower.

At times fog rises up above the ground to form a stratus cloud.

Upslope fogs can cause problems for mountain climbers trying to find their way.

Haze is often visible in the distance on warm, humid days.

If you wake up on a summer morning and it's foggy outside, don't worry. It will probably turn into a sunny day. Summer fogs usually mean there are few clouds in the sky above. Clouds hold down heat. They keep nighttime temperatures from dropping low enough for water droplets to condense into fog. But heat drifts away from the earth when the night sky is clear. The temperature may then drop enough for water vapor to condense into fog.

Haze is similar to fog but not as thick. Although most haze is composed of water droplets, it may consist of any kind of particles that make distant objects look fuzzy.

What Is Air Pollution?

Air pollution occurs when cars or other machines put smoke, dust, or some other substance into the atmosphere. The pollution may cause a brown, white, or gray haze to settle on the land. Sometimes pollution consists of gases and particles you can't see. Pollution can smell bad, burn your eyes, and make breathing hard, especially for people with lung problems. It may cause chest pains, nausea, coughing, and heart trouble.

Polluted air may stick around for days until a storm comes through and blows it away.

A haze of pollution limits visibility.

Oil refineries such as this are one source of air pollution.

Austin Post, US Geological Survey.

Even when a volcano isn't erupting, water vapor may escape from its top and condense into clouds.

In 1980, Oregon's Mount St. Helens volcano spewed gases and ash into the sky. *Inset:* Ash from the Mount St. Helens eruption darkened Kansas skies more than 1,000 miles (1,600km) away.

Smoke may cause the sun to appear orange or red even at midday, as it did here during the great Yellowstone Fires of 1988.

Do Volcanic Ash and Forest Fire Smoke Affect the Sky?

Volcanoes spew out a fine white powder called volcanic ash. Ash from a large volcanic eruption may darken the sky hundreds or even thousands of miles away. Volcanoes also produce gases that combine with water vapor to form a haze high above the earth. Volcanic material in the atmosphere filters sunlight and may cause our sunrises and sunsets to become redder than usual.

Smoke from forest fires may also darken faraway skies. In addition, heat from the fires creates updrafts that lift water vapor into the sky where it cools and condenses into cumulus, or sometimes cumulonimbus clouds.

Crepuscular rays look closer together in the distance, the way railroad tracks look closer near the horizon. They are actually parallel—the same distance apart along their entire lengths.

Trees filter sunlight to create crepuscular rays just as mountains, clouds, and buildings do.

What Are Those Bright Bands, Ribbons, and Columns I See in the Sky?

When mountains, buildings, or the uneven edges of a cloud block some of the sun's light, the light that isn't blocked shines through onto dust and other particles in the air. Millions of particles, all lit up at once, appear as bright bands of light called **crepuscular rays**. "Crepuscular" means "having to do with twilight." And twilight, when the sun is below the horizon, is one of the best times to see them. However, these rays may also shoot across the sky when the sun is above the horizon.

Sometimes clouds scatter light to form bright ribbons called **silver linings**. Silver linings appear only where the cloud is thin enough to let the light pass through—usually at the cloud edges.

Around sunrise or sunset, a single column of light may stretch from the sun into the sky. In this case, sunlight isn't being bent, as it is with most of the other light shows in the sky. This **sun pillar** is created by high-altitude ice crystals reflecting the light.

The dark bands between crepuscular rays are shadows cast by the clouds blocking sunlight.

Silver linings form when the sun is behind a cloud and water droplets at the cloud edges scatter the light.

A cloud with a silver lining may also produce crepuscular rays.

NOAA

A sun pillar is the same color as the sun, because the sunlight is reflected, not bent into different colors.

People used to say crepuscular rays were soaking up water for the next rain.

49

Is the Atmosphere the Same Everywhere?

Changes in temperature, humidity, precipitation, cloud cover, and other things that affect our weather, occur in the **troposphere**—the layer of the atmosphere right next to the earth. The troposphere contains four-fifths of all the air in the atmosphere. Above it lies the **stratosphere**. The stratosphere contains little air and almost no weather.

With so much going on in the troposphere, you'd think it would have to be thick. It isn't—just five miles (8km) deep at the poles and eleven miles (17km) at the equator. That's just a fraction of the total thickness of

Only the tops of the highest cumulonimbus clouds may reach above the troposphere and enter the bottom of the stratosphere.

It's colder in the mountains than in the lowlands, because the troposphere's temperature drops about 5 degrees Fahrenheit (3 degrees Celsius) for every 1,000 feet (300m).

50

the atmosphere—approximately 80 miles (128km). Most commercial jetliners fly no higher than about 6 or 7 miles (10 or 11km).

The air molecules in the troposphere group themselves into **air masses**—big blobs of air, hundreds, or even thousands of miles across. Temperature and humidity are nearly the same throughout an air mass at the same altitude. Air masses constantly form and disappear. Pushed by the wind, they bump into each other as they move across the earth's surface. When an air mass moves in from somewhere else, it may bring with it the temperature and humidity of the place in which it formed.

Weather occurs largely because the sun's heat warms the earth's surface and the troposphere.

Warm, dry air masses form over deserts. But wet air masses moving from the ocean may bring rain showers.

During the winter, cold, wet air masses from oceans near the north and south poles may bring snow to the continents.

Low pressure areas are often stormy.

High pressure air has few clouds and produces little precipitation.

People seem to be more alert and energetic when the air pressure is high and the weather is sunny.

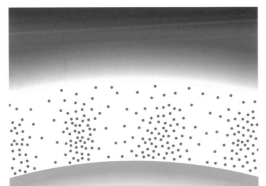

Think of the dots as molecules. There are more molecules near the center of each air mass than at the edges. That's why the air pressure is higher in the center.

Weather Reports Talk about High and Low Pressure. What Does that Mean?

The center of an air mass contains more molecules than the outer edges. This makes the center heavier than the edges. Heavier air exerts more pressure than lighter air. So an area of high pressure forms in the center of the air mass. The heavy, high pressure air sinks and its temperature rises. As the air gets warmer, there are fewer clouds. Without clouds, there can be no rain or snow.

Birds fly less in low pressure areas, possibly because when the air molecules are farther apart, the air doesn't hold the birds up as well.

At the edges of an air mass there are fewer molecules. This makes the air lighter. Lighter air exerts less pressure. The light, low pressure air floats up into the sky and cools. If it cools to its dew point, clouds form. The clouds may bring rain or snow. That's why storms are more common at the low pressure edges of an air mass than at its high pressure center.

If you like clear skies and sunny weather better than cloudy skies and rainy weather, here's one way to remember what high and low pressure mean. Think of the "h" in "high pressure" as standing for "happy weather," and of the "l" in "low pressure" as standing for "lousy weather."

The high pressure air over this city makes the mountains and houses look fuzzy and far away.

The dust-free air before a storm makes the mountains look clearer and closer.

Why Is the Air Often Clear Before a Storm?

Low pressure air usually contains little dust. If you look at distant hills or buildings through low pressure air, they look clearer and closer. Often, when the air pressure drops, a storm is on the way. So when objects look clear and close, it may mean rain or snow is coming. Sailors noticed this fact and put it in a rhyme:

> "The farther the sight
> The nearer the rain."

High pressure air is often dusty, which may make objects in the distance look fuzzy and farther away. High pressure skies are also usually sunny with few clouds. So in fair weather, distant objects often don't look sharp.

Where Does the Wind Come From?

Air molecules move farther apart as the air gets warmer. This makes the air lighter. Its pressure drops and it floats upward. Something has to replace it, so heavier, higher pressure air flows in to take its place. This flowing air is the wind. The wind always blows horizontally across the earth's surface. And it always blows from high pressure to low pressure.

The greater the difference between high pressure and low pressure air, the faster the wind blows, and the faster these wind turbines generate electricity.

Friction with the earth's surface causes the wind to move more slowly. But about half a mile (about 0.8 km) up, the surface has no effect on wind speed. This is the upper atmosphere. Here the winds are free to blow fast. Upper atmosphere winds above most of the world's people always blow more or less from the west to the east. That's why these great air movements are called the **westerly winds**. The "westerlies" cause much of the world's clouds and weather to come from the west and move toward the east.

Unlike the westerly winds, local, low altitude winds change direction from season to season and day to day.

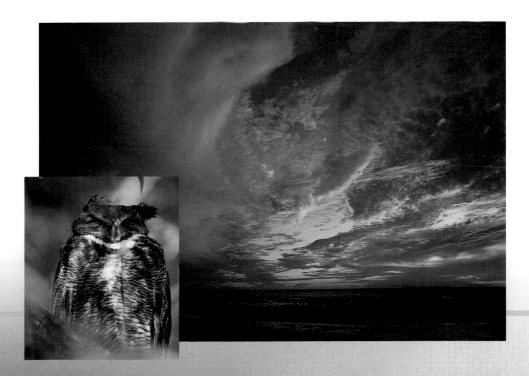

Small, local winds, like the one blowing on this owl (inset), and big, upper atmosphere winds pushing the clouds, both occur because some parts of the atmosphere warm up more than other parts do.

Is the Saying "Red Sky in the Morning, Sailors Take Warning" True?

The saying:

> "Red sky in the morning, sailors take warning.
> Red sky at night, sailors delight."

is one of the most accurate weather rhymes. To understand why, you need to know three things. First, dust turns the sky a pale shade of red when the sun is near the horizon. Second, dry air contains lots of dust. Third, the sun rises in the east and sets in the west.

If the setting sun colors the western sky red as night approaches, the air in that part of the sky is probably dry and dusty. You can expect the westerlies to carry that dry air from the west toward you. For sailors, dry air is a delight. It means they won't have to deal with rain while they're out at sea.

The "red sky" saying is correct about four out of five times.

European seamen started using the "Red sky" rhyme many years ago.

56

If the rising sun reddens the eastern sky in the morning, you know that the westerlies have already blown dry, dusty air away from you to the east. Bad weather often follows good weather. So the sight of dry air blowing away to the east warned sailors that wet air and a storm might be on the way.

Midwestern American farmers had their own saying:

Evening red and morning gray,
　　sets the traveler on his way.
Evening gray and morning red,
　　brings down rain upon his head.

The red sky part refers to dry air. The gray sky means cloudy, rainy air. If the morning is gray, the westerlies may blow the wet weather away to the east. But a gray evening sky may mean the westerlies are bringing in a storm.

The second part of the "red sky" saying is true more often than the first part, because dusty, dry air to the west will definitely blow your way—thanks to the westerly winds.

A red sky in the morning doesn't guarantee wet weather. The westerlies may bring more dry air.

A gray sky on the western horizon may mean that the westerlies are blowing in wet weather.

57

A low sun causes a rainbow arch to be high and steep.

The higher the sun, the flatter the rainbow. When the sun is very high a rainbow flattens so much you can't see it.

Most rainbows aren't full arches, because clouds block some of the sunlight needed to strike enough raindrops at the correct angle to form a full arch.

The sun is in the right position to form a rainbow only within three hours after sunrise and three hours before sunset.

EXPERIMENT

Make A Rainbow

With your back to the sun, squirt a fine spray of drops from a garden hose. Move the hose around until you see a rainbow. Change the size of the drops by adjusting the spray nozzle. Small drops are best for making rainbows. Large drops flatten out as they fall and don't reflect colors as well as small, round drops do.

If you use a hose to make a rainbow, don't waste the water. Spray it on plants.

Can You Find the End of the Rainbow?

Like little prisms, raindrops may bend and separate sunlight into different colors as a rainbow. Each raindrop in a rainbow reflects all the colors in sunlight, but each color is reflected at a different angle. The red comes from drops that reflect the red part of the light in exactly your direction. That same drop reflects the other colors too, but they aren't heading toward you at an angle you can see. The orange you see comes from a totally different set of drops. And the yellow comes from other drops. Still other drops reflect the other colors at just the right angle to reach your eyes. Someone standing next to you sees what looks like the same rainbow you see. But the colors that person sees are reflected by different drops. That's why no two people see exactly the same rainbow.

Have you ever tried to walk up to a rainbow? You can't. A rainbow exists only because you are at a certain angle and distance from the sun and the raindrops. Every step you take toward a rainbow changes that angle and distance. You may still see a rainbow. But it's coming from drops that are a little farther away.

Rainbows usually appear with cumulonimbus, not nimbostratus clouds.

Rainbows in the mist around waterfalls form in the same way rainbows in the sky do.

Look for rainbows in the eastern sky following afternoon showers, because cumulonimbus clouds usually form in the afternoon and move from west to east.

59

In a double rainbow, the primary bow is always brighter and clearer than the secondary bow.

In a secondary rainbow, violet is on the outside and red is on the inside—just the opposite of the primary rainbow.

The two rainbows in a double rainbow reflect no light between them, causing this area to be darker. If the rainbow is single, the sky outside the arch is darker.

What about Double Rainbows?

With luck, you'll get to see a double rainbow. The inner one is called the primary rainbow or primary bow. The outer one is the secondary rainbow or secondary bow. This double bonus forms as raindrops bend and reflect sunlight twice.

The order of colors in both a single rainbow and a primary rainbow from outside to inside is red, orange, yellow, green, blue, indigo, and violet. Red is on the outer edge and violet is on the inner edge because raindrops bend violet the most and red the least. But in a secondary rainbow, the color order is reversed.

Why Do People Say "Mountains Make Their Own Weather"?

The land in a rain shadow may be very dry, even though nearby mountains receive lots of precipitation.

When air rises up a mountainside it cools about five degrees Fahrenheit (three degrees Celsius) for every 1,000 feet (300m). Eventually, the temperature of the air drops to its dew point and its water vapor condenses into clouds. This explains why the windward sides of mountains—the sides facing the dominant winds—are some of the cloudiest and rainiest places on earth.

After mountain winds drop much of their moisture on a mountain's windward side, they are quite dry as they blow down the **leeward** side—the side facing away from the wind. Compared to the windward side of a mountain, the leeward slopes, valleys, and lowlands receive little precipitation. They are in the mountain's **rain shadow**.

It may be warm and sunny back home, but when you visit the mountains, there are often clouds and precipitation.

Mountain skies are often a deep shade of blue, because they contain fewer particles to scatter sunlight.

Weather Forecasters Talk about "Fronts"— What Are They?

Air masses rarely mix unless their temperature and humidity are almost the same. Instead, a boundary forms between them called a **front**. Fronts may be hundreds of miles long. The air mass with the lower temperature is called the cold air mass. The one with the higher temperature is the warm air mass. The warm air always rises up and over the cold air, because warm air weighs less.

The direction of the wind often changes when a front passes through.

Because air masses touch each other at their low pressure edges, fronts are the centers of large low pressure areas. Low pressure can mean stormy weather. Just as army battles take place along military fronts, battles in the form of storms take place along the fronts between air masses. If the warm air moves forward and the cold air moves back, the front is called a **warm front**. But if the cold air advances while the warm air retreats, it's a **cold front**.

A cold front speeds along at up to 30 miles (48km) per hour—much faster than a warm front. The cold air wedges under the warm air and shoves it up into the sky, because warm air weighs less. As the warm air quickly rises, its temperature plunges to the dew point and clouds appear.

The first signs of a cold front may be the cumulus clouds that often show up during fair weather. But as the cold front charges closer, other clouds such as nimbostratus or cumulonimbus may appear. Rain, snow, or hail may follow, sometimes with thunder and lightning. Violent storms are typical of a strong cold front. An unbroken chain of fast-moving thunderstorms, parallel to the edge of a cold front, is called a **squall line**.

As a cold front approaches, the warm air mass rises rapidly up and over the cold air mass.

The clear skies and cold temperatures following a cold front may last until another front comes along.

A wall of growing cumulus clouds may signal the approach of a cold front.

NOAA

The dark, threatening clouds of a squall line may be more than 100 miles (160km) long and often from 50 miles (80km) to 150 miles (240km) ahead of an advancing cold front.

Mares' tails or cirrus clouds may be the first signs of an approaching warm front.

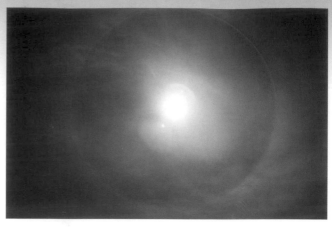

As a warm front nears, a cirrostratus layer may form a halo around the sun.

A mackerel sky of altocumulus clouds replaces the cirrostratus layer brought in by a warm front.

The mackerel sky is followed by a darkening altostratus layer that dims the sun and makes it look "wet."

As the slope of a warm front nears ground level, the cloud ceiling lowers into a stratus layer, which may turn into a nimbostratus if precipitation falls.

Wet weather brought by a warm front may last a few days. Afterwards, temperatures rise and the skies clear.

How Can I Tell When a Warm Front Is Passing Through?

The high point of a warm front may be 25,000 feet (7,600m) above the earth and hundreds of miles ahead of the point where the front contacts the ground.

A warm front moves slowly at about 15 miles (24km) per hour—half the speed of a cold front. The clouds that come with it are high at first but get lower as the front gets closer. Cirrus clouds or mares' tails appear first, up to two days before the front reaches you. As the warm front moves closer, the cirrus streaks thicken into cirrostratus clouds, which may produce a halo. Halos may be warnings that wet weather is coming, as told in the rhyme:

"Ring around the moon, rain by noon.
Ring around the sun, rain before night is done."

As the warm front advances, mid-level altocumulus clouds may replace the cirrostratus to create a mackerel sky. Sailors used to say, "Mares' tails and mackerel skies make tall ships take in their sails." They knew that mares' tails followed by mackerel skies could warn of a storm—and it was not a good time for a ship to have its sails up.

As the front inches on, the sun dims into a bright spot behind a thickening gray or blue-gray blanket of altostratus clouds. By the time a warm front reaches you, a low, stratus layer covers the sky. It may get darker and lower, turning into nimbostratus, sometimes with a cumulonimbus higher up. Then rain or snow falls.

A warm front may not bring all of these clouds. And some may appear without having anything to do with a front. But if the clouds get lower and darker, you know that wet weather is possible.

What Are Northern and Southern Lights?

People who live in the far north and south frequently enjoy fantastic shows of colored lights dancing across the night skies. The northern lights go by the name Aurora Borealis and the southern lights are called Aurora Australis. Sometimes scientists refer to both as the Aurora Polaris. More often, they just say "the auroras."

The auroras occur much higher than clouds—50 to 600 miles (80 to 1,000km) above the earth. Auroras aren't made of water droplets or ice crystals, as clouds are. They form because of the **solar wind**, tiny particles that stream out from the sun. The particles bombard gas molecules in the atmosphere near the North and South Poles. The collisions give off the auroras' glowing arches, bands, streamers, and curtains of red, yellow, and green.

NOAA

Usually, only people in the northern part of the Northern Hemisphere and southern part of the Southern Hemisphere see auroras.

NOAA

Auroras may remain still, or they may move and ripple. They may last minutes or hours.

When the solar wind is very strong, people in places other than the far north and south may see the auroras.

NOAA

Sunlight reflected by the moon takes about one-and-one-quarter seconds to reach our eyes.

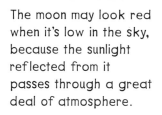

The moon may look red when it's low in the sky, because the sunlight reflected from it passes through a great deal of atmosphere.

Sometimes the moon is up during the day. But it's easier to see when it's up during the night.

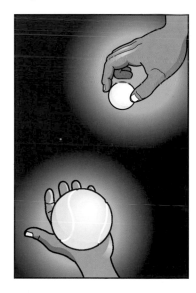

Each day the moon rises fifty minutes later than the day before.

Why Is the Moon White, and Why Does It Look So Big?

We see the big ball of rock we call the moon because of the white sunlight reflected from its surface. Because the earth is always turning, the moon appears to rise and set just as the sun does.

The moon is one quarter the size of the earth. As it sits in the sky, the moon seems to be the same size as the sun even though the moon is actually hundreds of times smaller. The moon looks so big because it's so close—just a quarter million miles (about 400,000km) away, while the sun is 93 million miles (150 million km) away.

If the earth were the size of a tennis ball, the moon, would be more like a ping-pong ball.

Why Does the Moon Seem to Change Shape?

Although the moon orbits—moves around—the earth, the side of the moon facing us never changes. But the amount of sunlight hitting our side of the moon does change throughout each month. When the moon is on the same side of the earth as the sun is, no sunlight hits the side facing us and we can't see it. This is the new moon. But a day or two later, as the moon moves on, a crescent moon appears because sunlight falls on less than half of our side of the moon.

After a week, the moon has completed the first quarter of its monthly orbit. Now the moon is in its first quarter phase and half the side facing us is lit up.

A little later, we see a gibbous moon when more than half, but not all of the side facing us is illuminated.

Our side of the moon is completely visible during the full moon phase because the sun and moon are on opposite sides of the earth. A full moon is halfway through its monthly orbit.

Within days, a gibbous moon appears once again.

This is followed by the last quarter phase, when the lunar orbit is three-quarters complete and half of our side of the moon receives

Waxing crescent moon.

Waxing first quarter moon.

Full moon.

Waning gibbous moon.

sunlight. The cycle ends with another crescent.

A **waxing moon** is changing from new to full. A waning moon changes from full to new. Sometimes you can see the dark part of the moon during the new and crescent phases because of **earthshine**. That is, a small amount of sunlight reflects off the earth and shines up onto the moon.

Earthshine. If you look closely, you will see the shape of a full moon.

Occasionally the earth gets between the sun and moon and casts its shadow on the moon's face. This is a lunar eclipse. When only part of earth's shadow darkens the moon, it's a partial lunar eclipse. During a total lunar eclipse, earth's shadow darkens the moon completely.

A solar eclipse occurs when the moon passes between the earth and the sun. The sun seems to turn black and a shadow darkens the earth.

The moon gradually appears smaller as the earth's shadow passes over it during an eclipse.

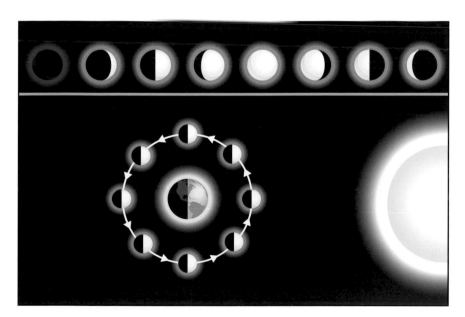

The moon's orbit around the earth and relationship to the sun.

What Am I Looking at When I Look at the Stars?

When you look at the closest star to earth—other than our sun—you are seeing what it looked like four years ago. That's because this star, called Proxima Centauri, is 20 trillion miles (30 trillion km) or four light-years from earth. One light-year is the distance light travels in one year. The very farthest stars scientists know of are billions of light-years away. You can't see most of them without a telescope.

Ancient people thought the stars formed patterns, and they named them for mythological characters, animals, and objects. These patterns are called constellations.

If you point a camera at the North Star, and hold the camera's shutter open for a long time, the other stars will leave circular trails on the film around the North Star as the earth turns.

"The Big Dipper" is a constellation shaped like a dipper for dipping up water. No matter where the Big Dipper is in the sky, the two end stars of its bowl always point to the North Star.

If you watch the stars long enough, you'll see that they seem to move slowly across the sky. Actually, we're the ones who are moving, because the earth is always turning. In the Northern Hemisphere, the North Star moves less than all the other stars. It's always due north because it sits above the earth's axis, the imaginary line the earth turns around.

You may also notice that some stars give off colors. The hottest stars have a blue tone. Stars that aren't as hot give off more red light. White and yellow stars have temperatures in between the hot blue stars and the cooler red ones.

The three stars in a row in the center of the photo make up the belt of Orion, The Hunter, one of the 88 constellations.

Unlike stars, planets produce no light of their own. We see them because of the sunlight they reflect. Planets don't twinkle like stars do. Twinkling occurs because air currents in our atmosphere bounce the starlight around. The light from planets gets bounced around too, but since planets are so big, we don't notice any twinkling.

In the Southern Hemisphere, there is a constellation of four bright stars that is called the Southern Cross. The cross's longest arm always points south.

What Are Shooting Stars and Stars with Tails?

At some point during your life, you may be treated to a rare sight— a star with a tail. But it isn't a star; it's a comet. Comets have been called big, dirty snowballs. They're chunks of rock and ice, 20 feet (6m) to hundreds of miles across, which orbit the sun in oval-shaped paths. When a comet is near the sun, some of its ice turns into glowing gases. The gases are blown into a long tail by the solar wind. A large comet tail may stretch millions of miles through space.

Have you ever been startled by a streak of light shooting across the night sky and called it a shooting star? That isn't a star either; it's a meteor. Meteors come from meteoroids, pieces of rock, dust, or ice speeding through space. When a meteoroid hits the earth's atmosphere, it pushes rapidly into it. So much friction builds up as it crashes through the air molecules, that the meteoroid bursts into flame. The burning, glowing meteoroid is now called a meteor.

Keith Cooper

In 1996 and 1997, the Hale Bopp comet was clearly visible from Earth.

72

To see meteors, get far away from bright lights and look into the night sky for at least half an hour. Choose a time when there are few clouds and little or no moon, preferably after midnight. Most meteors burn up and disappear about 50 or 60 miles (80.5km or 96.5km) above the earth. But some hit the earth's surface. At that point they are called meteorites.

As comets orbit the sun, ice and dust from their tails may fly into the earth's atmosphere as meteor showers. Meteor showers from different comets occur at definite times each year. Below is a list of some of the major meteor showers.

Delta-Aquarids	July 25–August 8	up to 10 to 35 meteors per hour
Perseids	August 11–13	up to 50 to 100 meteors per hour
Orionids	October 20–23	up to 10 to 70 meteors per hour
Taurids	November 5–17	up to 5 to 15 meteors per hour
Leonids	November 16–18	number varies from year to year
Geminids	December 11–14	up to 50 to 80 meteors per hour

Unlike a comet that sits in the sky night after night, a meteor such as this one usually appears for less than a second.

Meteor Crater Enterprise

About 40,000 years ago, a large meteor struck the earth and left this crater in what is now Arizona.

From an airplane, you can see sky signs such as these cumulus clouds (left) and stratocumulus clouds (right) in a whole different way.

How Can I Become Sky-Wise?

Benjamin Franklin once said, "Some people are weather-wise. But most are otherwise." In Ben Franklin's day, there were no weather reports. To be "weather-wise" you had to read what the sky had to say about the coming weather. You had to be sky-wise. Today, you can learn all kinds of things about the sky from books. But to become truly sky-wise, you also need to spend time looking at the sky. You may want to take a sky photo from the same place every day in the morning and evening, and compare each photo to the official weather report for that day.

As you learn more, you'll realize how small we are compared to the sky. And what about outer space? Where does it end? This may lead you to ask things like "who are we in this big universe anyway?" And "why are we here?" These are tough questions. But, perhaps, the more you learn, the closer you'll be to the answers. Just remember, keep looking up.

A pair of binoculars gives you a great view of the clouds, the moon's surface, and star color. Just don't look at the sun!

Glossary

Afterglow. Light from the sun between sunset and full night.

Air masses. Big blobs of air in which the temperature and humidity are nearly the same at the same altitude.

Air. The mixture of gases surrounding the earth.

Altocumulus clouds. Puffy, middle level clouds that form in air made unstable by rising air currents.

Altostratus clouds. Middle level cloud layers that form in stable air.

Anvil. Fan-like structure of ice crystals at the top of a tall cumulonimbus cloud.

Cirrocumulus clouds. High, small, puffy, ice crystal clouds that form in unstable air.

Cirrostratus clouds. High, thin, ice crystal cloud layers that form in stable air.

Cirrus clouds. High, thin, wispy, ice crystal clouds.

Cold front. The boundary between a colder air mass pushing a warmer air mass.

Contrail. The trail of water vapor from a jet engine exhaust frozen into ice crystals at high altitudes.

Corona. A small, bright, and often colorful disk around the sun or moon caused when water droplets in middle level clouds bend light.

Crepuscular rays. Bright bands of light caused when mountains, buildings, trees, or the uneven edges of a cloud block some of the sun's light.

Cumulonimbus clouds. Cumulus clouds that produce rain or snow.

Cumulus clouds. Low, puffy, water droplet clouds.

Dew point. The temperature at which water vapor starts to condense into water droplets.

Earthshine. The small amount of sunlight reflected from Earth to the dark part of the Moon when the Moon is in the New or Crescent phases.

Fog. A cloud at ground level.

Front. A boundary between air masses, often the site of storms.

Hailstones. Ice balls of various sizes that fall from tall cumulonimbus clouds.

Halo. A large ring around the sun or moon formed when the ice crystals in a cirrostratus cloud bend light.

Haze. Water droplets or other particles, smaller than those in fog, which make distant objects look fuzzy.

Hemispheres. The two halves of the earth (Northern Hemisphere and Southern Hemisphere) on either side of the equator.

Humidity. The amount of water vapor in the air.

Iridescence. A patch of color on the bottom of middle level clouds caused when the cloud's water droplets of the same size bend sunlight.

Leeward. Facing away from the direction the wind is blowing from.

Mammatus. Bag-like bulges pushed by strong downdrafts at the bottom of a big cumulonimbus cloud.

Morning glow. The light in the sky between full night and sunrise.

Nimbostratus clouds. Stratus clouds that produce rain or snow.

Precipitation. Rain, snow, or other form of water that falls from the sky.

Rain shadow. The leeward slopes, valleys, and lowlands of a mountain or mountain range that receive little precipitation.

Scuds. Cloud pieces formed when falling rain evaporates and saturates the air below a rain cloud with water vapor.

Silver linings. Bright ribbons of light that appear where the cloud is thin enough to let the light pass through, usually at the cloud edges.

Solar wind. Tiny particles streaming out from the sun.

Squall line. An unbroken line of severe thunderstorms that may come in front of a fast-moving cold front.

Stratocumulus clouds. Low, water droplet clouds that form lumpy, wavy, or slightly puffy cloud layers.

Stratosphere. The layer of the atmosphere above the troposphere, containing little air and almost no weather.

Stratus clouds. Flat, layer-like clouds from ground level up to about one-half mile (0.8 km).

Sun dogs. Bright spots, sometimes colorful, that sit on opposite sides of a halo.

Sun pillar. A column of light reflected from the sun by high altitude ice crystals near sunrise or sunset.

Supercells. Big, powerful, long-lasting thunderstorms caused when the updrafts in big cumulonimbus clouds turn in rotating patterns.

Thermal. Warm air that rises due to sunlight heating the earth's surface.

Thunderheads. A big cumulonimbus cloud that produces thunder and lightning.

Tornado. A funnel-shaped cloud that forms a violent, whirling wind storm.

Troposphere. Layer of the atmosphere next to the earth.

Twilight. That time of day when the sun isn't in the sky but there is still light.

Virga. Rain or snow falling from a cloud that evaporates before reaching the earth.

Warm front. The boundary between a warmer air mass pushing a colder air mass.

Water vapor. The gas form of water.

Waterspout. A funnel-shaped cloud of whirling winds on water.

Wave clouds. Smooth, streamlined clouds that form when middle level winds flow in up-and-down wave patterns.

Westerly winds. Upper atmosphere winds blowing from west to east.

Index

About the Author

Marsha Kinkade

Frank Staub is a photographer and writer specializing in nature, foreign cultures, and adventure sports. His photographs have been featured in over 30 books on subjects ranging from manatees to mountain goats and from Yucatan to the Yellowstone Fires. He also wrote most of these books, and has received seven national awards. His photographs have appeared in dozens of other publications and he has authored numerous magazine articles and audiovisual productions. He holds a bachelor's degree in biology from Muhlenberg College, a master's degree in zoology from the University of Rhode Island, and has worked as a whitewater river guide, truck driver, railroad track laborer, veterinary assistant, and high school science teacher. He lives in Tucson, Arizona, and spends his free time bicycling, hiking, diving, sea kayaking, and climbing mountains.